MANATEES

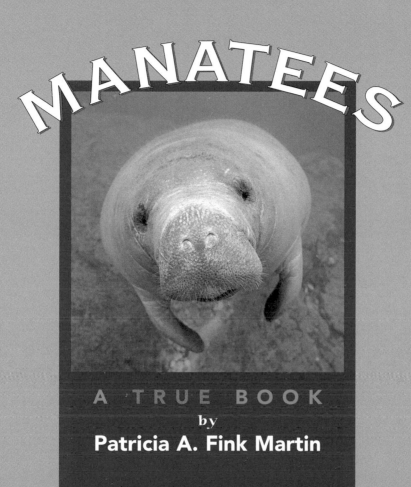

A TRUE BOOK

by

Patricia A. Fink Martin

Children's Press®

A Division of Scholastic Inc.

New York Toronto London Auckland Sydney
Mexico City New Delhi Hong Kong
Danbury, Connecticut

People like to
watch manatees.

Reading Consultant
Nanci R. Vargus, Ed.D.
Primary Multiage Teacher
Decatur Township Schools,
Indianapolis, IN

Content Consultant
Kathy Carlstead, Ph.D.
Honolulu Zoo

Library of Congress Cataloging-in-Publication Data

Martin, Patricia A. Fink.
    Manatees / by Patricia A. Fink Martin.
        p. cm. – (A True book)
    Includes bibliographical references and index.
    Summary: Describes the physical characteristics, behavior, habitat, and
endangered status of the manatees.
    ISBN 0-516-22163-9 (lib. bdg.)   0-516-27473-2 (pbk.)
    1. Manatees—Juvenile literature. [1. Manatees. 2. Endangered
species.] I. Title. II. Series.
QL737.S63 M364 2002
599.55—dc21
                                                                    2001032301

13 14 15 16 17 18 19 20 21 R 17 16 15 14 13 12   08

Contents

Many years ago, people believed that mermaids swam in the sea.

Living Mermaids

Long ago, people believed in mermaids. They built statues of them. Sailors searched for mermaids on their long ocean voyages. Some people even believed they'd seen mermaids. Today we know that mermaids aren't real. But what did those sailors really see?

Manatees were once mistaken for mermaids.

Some people think they saw animals called **sirenians**.

Sirenians are **mammals** that spend their lives under-water in rivers and oceans. Like dolphins, whales, and other water mammals, they breathe air. Sirenians grow to be quite large, with most of them growing to more than 10 feet (3 meters) long. Some can weigh as much as 3,000 pounds (1,360 kilograms).

The most common sirenian is the manatee, or sea cow. Manatees don't look much like mermaids. In fact, a manatee's

The manatee is the most common type of sirenian.

A manatee
has a very
large snout.

body is shaped like a baked
potato. Its skin is gray and
wrinkled, with a few stiff hairs.
A broad, whiskered snout

takes up most of its face. On top of its snout sit two small nostrils. Tiny dark eyes lie far apart above the nostrils.

Many times, only the manatee's two small nostrils come above water.

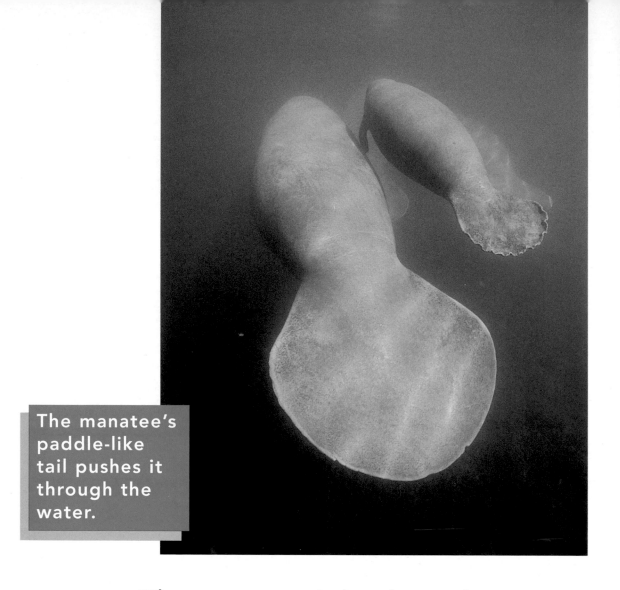

The manatee's paddle-like tail pushes it through the water.

The manatee's body ends in a paddle-like tail. Two flippers stick out from each side, just

Flippers help a manatee steer its body.

behind its head. The tail pushes the manatee through the water. Its flippers help it steer.

Manatee

African elephant

Manatees don't look much like elephants, but elephants may be the manatees' closest relatives that live on land. Scientists have found that these two animals share common blood substances. In addition, the shapes of their skulls and lower jaws are similar. The skin of the elephant is much like that of the manatee. Both animals have rough, gray skin with a few hairs. Have you ever noticed an elephant's foot? It doesn't have claws like many mammals do. Instead, it has flat nails.

Relatives

Dugong

Manatees also have flat nails at the end of each flipper.

The second manatee relative swims in the Indian and Pacific Oceans. This animal, called the dugong, has a body that is shaped like the body of the manatee. But the dugong's skin is smooth. The tail end of the dugong is flattened, and it isn't round like the manatee tail. The dugong's tail is split into left and right parts. Its tail looks like that of a whale or dolphin. The dugong feeds on plants that grow on the bottom of the ocean.

A Watery Home

Manatees live mostly in the hot or tropical parts of the world. They like shallow, slow-moving water. Some swim in fresh water, but others prefer ocean water. Many swim in both environments.

Some manatees live as far away as western Africa. Another group can be found in the rivers

Manatees swim in both fresh and salt water.

of central South America. A third kind of manatee can be found closer to home. This kind, called the West Indian manatee, lives along the coasts of the

Caribbean islands and the tip of South America. It also lives along Florida's coast and rivers.

Would you like to see a manatee? In Florida, you can view these water giants in lots of places. In the summer, you can find them in the ocean. Some live in rivers close by. During cold weather, you'll find them in **springs**, rivers, and along the coast near power plants. Power plants release a lot of warm water into nearby bodies of water.

MANATEE
VIEWING AREA
NO FISHING OR
BANK ACCESS

People come to viewing areas to watch manatees.

Living Underwater

Manatees do almost everything underwater. They eat, sleep, and play there. They also have their babies underwater. But remarkably, they can't breathe underwater.

Manatees breathe air just like we do. Almost every 2 to 4 minutes, a manatee rises to

A manatee can do everything underwater except breathe.

the water's surface. It pokes only its nose above the water. The manatee opens each nostril to breathe. As the manatee sinks, its nostril flaps close.

A manatee rises to the surface for a breath of fresh air.

Can you hold your breath for 2 minutes? A baby manatee can't. It comes up every 30 seconds to get a breath. It has to learn how to breathe like an adult manatee.

Manatees sleep underwater. In nice weather, they lay on their backs on the bottom. Some rest on their stomachs. In cold weather they float just below the surface of the water.

Manatees sleep on the bottom of a river.

Even asleep, they must breathe. A sleeping manatee rises to the surface every 20 minutes. It takes a breath, then it slowly sinks back down.

Manatees also eat under-water, munching on grasses and other water plants. A large manatee eats almost 100 pounds (45 kg) of plants in a day! But they don't just eat the leaves and stems— they like the roots of some plants too.

Water plants and grasses are a manatee's favorite food.

To find buried roots, a manatee digs in the mud with its flippers.

Manatees grab leaves with their big lips. They use their flippers too. They can dig into the sand and mud where they find roots and underground stems. Their big back teeth grind up the food.

A Manatee Journey

Manatees swim from one feeding spot to another. They don't go far as they search for food. They swim slowly, moving about 2 to 5 miles (3 to 8 kilometers) per hour. In a day, a manatee may swim only a few miles.

But twice a year manatees take long journeys. In the winter

Manatees migrate to warmer waters in the winter.

Special tags on a manatee's tail tell scientists where the animal is.

they **migrate** to warmer waters. In the spring they leave their warm-water **refuges**. Some travel to the ocean or along the coast, while others move upriver. Manatees look for good feeding grounds.

How do scientists study these journeys? They attach special tags to a manatee's tail. Some tags send radio signals back to the scientists. One thing they have learned is that manatees travel alone or in small groups.

Cows and Calves

An adult manatee spends most of its life alone. But at times, males and females come together to mate. The males are called bulls and the female manatees are called cows. A group of males may follow a cow for days. When she is ready, she will mate. After that, the males leave.

Bulls and cows come together to mate.

About a year later the female has a baby manatee, which is called a calf. The calf is born underwater, and it weighs about 60 pounds (27 kg). Right away, it swims

A calf weighs about 60 pounds (27 kg) at birth.

Two calves are nursed by their mother.

to the surface to breathe. Its mother stays beside it. Within a few hours, the calf drinks its mother's milk.

Mother manatees take good care of their babies.

A cow nuzzles her calf with her snout.

The cow touches her calf often, nuzzling it with her big snout. Her baby swims close to her side. Sometimes it rests on her back. Cows and calves even talk to each other. Their talk sounds like chirps, whistles, and squeals to us.

The cow and calf stay together for two years. The cow teaches her calf what plants to eat and where to find food. In the winter, the pair migrates. In the spring, the cow and calf return to their summer home.

Manatees in Danger

Manatees are in danger. One day, there may be no more manatees. The manatee is listed as an **endangered species**. Many die each year from the things that humans do. Boats injure and kill manatees. Manatees swim slowly. When boats speed up, manatees

Manatees may one
day become extinct.

Speeding boats (above) do not give manatees enough time to move out of the way. Propeller cuts on a manatee's back (right)

can't get out of the way. Some are hit by the boat's hull, but more often the propeller cuts them. Most Florida manatees have cuts on their backs. Scientists know many manatees by these scars.

Some people still hunt manatees. Manatees can get caught in crab trap lines. They may lose a flipper or even die. In some of Florida's rivers, huge gates sit in the water. These gates open and close to control water levels. These moving gates can crush or kill manatees.

Saving the Manatees

Many people are working hard to save manatees. In the United States, several laws protect them. The state of Florida is asking boaters to slow down, and has posted speed limit signs to warn boaters about manatees. Special parks have also been set up for manatees.

Signs like this warn boaters to slow down and watch for manatees.

You too can help manatees. You can join the Save the Manatee Club and help raise money for their projects. You

Special areas have been set aside for manatees.

can even adopt a manatee.
Do you live in Florida? If you
do, ask your parents to buy
the manatee license plate.
Some of the money that you

pay for the special plates is used to help manatees. You do not have to do all of these things. Even one action can help.

Manatee license plates help raise money for the animals.

To Find Out More

If you'd like to learn more about manatees, check out these additional resources.

 **Books**

Corrigan, Patricia. **Manatees for Kids.** NorthSouth Books, 1996.

Darling, Kathy. **Manatees on Location.** Lothrop, Lee & Shepard Books, 1991.

Harman, Amanda. **Manatees and Dugongs.** Marshall Cavendish, 1997.

Johnston, Marianne. **Manatees.** PowerKids Press, 1997.

Silverstein, Alvin, Virginia and Robert, and Laura Silverstein Nunn. **The Manatee.** Millbrook Press, 1995.

Organizations and Online Sites

Blue Springs State Park
Orange City, FL 32763
http://www.dep.state.fl.us/ parks/Bluesprings/ bluespring.html

Visit this park between November and March to see the manatees.

Homosassa Springs Wildlife Park
4150 S. Suncoast Boulevard Homosassa Springs, FL 34446
http://www.nccentral.com/ hswildlife.htm

Don't miss the manatee cam! Here you can view manatees that live in the main spring.

Save the Manatee Club
500 N. Maitland Avenue Maitland, FL 32751
http://www.savethemanatee. org

Sea World of Florida
7007 Sea World Drive Orlando, FL 32809
http://www.seaworld.org/ manatee

Important Words

endangered species a living thing in danger of dying out

mammal an animal with a backbone that is covered with hair, is warm-blooded, and feeds its young milk

migrate to move, usually as a group, from one place to another far away, to mate or feed

refuge a safe or protected place to stay

sirenian a type of large mammal that lives in water; includes four living species: the West African manatee, the Amazonian manatee, the West Indian manatee, and the dugong

spring a place where water flows up from the ground year-round. The temperature of the water stays the same in summer or winter. In places such as Florida, spring water feels warmer than the air in winter.

Index

Meet the Author

Patricia A. Fink Martin holds a doctorate in biology. After spending many years teaching and working in the laboratory, she began writing science books for children. In 1998, *Booklist* chose her first book, *Animals that Walk on Water*, as one of the ten best animal books for children for that year. She has since published eight more books. Dr. Martin lives in Tennessee with her husband Jerry, their daughter Leslie, and their golden retriever Ginger.